# True Stories Pack 2
## Teaching Notes

*Thelma Page*

## Cor

### The King of Football
*The Story of Pelé*

### Arctic Hero
*The Story of Matthew Henson*

### Pioneer Girl
*The Story of Laura Ingalls Wilder*

### Man on the Moon
*The Story of Neil Armstrong*

### Titanic Survivor
*The Story of Harold Bride*

### Born to Dance
*The Story of Rudolf Nureyev*

# Welcome to Oxford Reading Tree True Stories!

This new set of stories at Stages 10 and 11 has been specially written to provide new biographies of fascinating lives. Children who prefer factual books to fiction will particularly welcome them. The stories also provide exciting narratives for those children who love fiction and need to be tempted to broaden their horizons.

In group and independent reading of these stories, the children are encouraged to develop their understanding and use of non-fiction texts by

- Clarifying their understanding of the difference between fact and fiction
- Learning to skim-read to find particular information
- Practising note-taking to use in their own writing
- Developing their ability to use their own words to give an oral or written report
- Developing their vocabulary and spelling strategies

The stories feature a range of men and women from various cultural backgrounds and from different times in history. In pack 2 the range is from Laura Ingalls Wilder, born in 1867, to heroes from the second half of the 20th century: Rudolf Nureyev, Pelé and Neil Armstrong. All the stories show that real life can be every bit as exciting as a fictional adventure.

## How to introduce the books

- Before reading the story, always read the title and talk about the picture on the cover. Find out what the children already know about the person featured. Read the blurb on the back cover.
- Go through the book together, looking at the pictures and talking about them.
- Read through the words in the glossary together. This lists technical and specialist words related to the person's life and achievements.

# Teaching objectives

## Curriculum coverage chart

| | Speaking and listening | Reading | Writing |
|---|---|---|---|
| **The King of Football** *The Story of Pelé* | | | |
| Scotland | Levels C | Levels C | Levels C |
| N. Ireland | Activities a,b,c,f,g,h,i Outcomes: abcdefg | Activities: a,b,c,e,f,h Outcomes: b,c,d,e,f,g, h,i,j,k | Outcomes: a,b,c,d,e,f,h,i |
| Wales | Range 1,2,3,5,6 Skills 1,2,3,4,5,6 Language Development: 1,2,3,4,5 | Range 1,2,3,4,6 Skills 1,2,4 Language Development: 1,2 | Range: 1,3,4,5,6,7 Skills: 1,2,4,5,6,7,8 Language Development: 1,2,3,4 |
| **NC KS2/NLS Y3T1** | 1c 2b 3d 4a | W9 S1 T19 | W5 |
| **Arctic Hero** *The Story of Matthew Henson* | | | |
| Scotland | Levels C | Levels C | Levels C |
| N. Ireland | Activities: a,b,c,f,g,h,i Outcomes: a,b,c,d,e,f,g | Activities: a,b,c,e,f,h Outcomes: b,c,d,e,f,g,i, j,k | Outcomes: a,b,c,d,e,f,h,i |
| Wales | Range 1,2,3,5,6 Skills: 1,2,3,4,5,6 Language Development: 1,2,3,4,5 | Range 1,2,3,4,6 Skills: 1,2,4 Language Development: 1,2 | Range 1,3,4,5,6,7 Skills: 1,2,4,5,6,7,8 Language Development: 1,2,3,4 |
| **NC KS2/NLS Y3T1** | 1c 2a 3b 4c | W8 S2 T1 | T13 |
| **Pioneer Girl** *The Story of Laura Ingalls Wilder* | | | |
| Scotland | Level C | Level C | Level C |
| N. Ireland | Activities: a,b,c,f,g,h,i Outcomes: a,b,c,d,e,f,g | Activities: a,b,c,e,f,h Outcomes: b,c,d,e,f,g, i,j,k | Outcomes: a,b,c,d,e,f,h,i |
| Wales | Range: 1,2,3,5 Skills: 1,2,3,4,5,6 Language Development: 1,2,3,4,5 | Range: 1,2,3,4,6 Skills: 1,2,4 Language Development: 1,2 | Range: 1,3,4,5,6,7 Skills: 1,2,4,5,6,7,8 Language Development: 1,2,3,4 |
| **NC KS2/NLS Y3T1** | 1a 2c 3a 4b | W8 S6 T3 | T17 |
| **Man on the Moon** *The Story of Neil Armstrong* | | | |
| Scotland | Level C | Level C | Level C |
| N. Ireland | Activities: a,b,c,f,g,h,i Outcomes: a,b,c,d,e,f,g | Activities: a,b,c,e,f,h Outcomes: b,c,d,e,f,g,h, i,j,k | Outcomes: a,b,c,d,e,f,h,i |
| Wales | Range: 1,2,3,5,6 Skills: 1,2,3,4,5,6 Language Development: 1,2,3,4,5 | Range: 1,2,3,4,6 Skills: 1,2,4 Language Development: 1,2 | Range: 1,3,4,5,6,7 Skills: 1,2,4,5,6,7,8 Language Development: 1,2,3,4 |
| **NC KS2/NLS Y3T1** | 1c 2b 3a 4a | W6 T5 T7 | T7 |

| Titanic Survivor *The Story of Harold Bride* | | | |
|---|---|---|---|
| Scotland | Level C | Level C | Level C |
| N. Ireland | Activities: a,b,c,f,g,h,i<br>Outcomes: a,b,c,d,e,f,g | Activities: a,b,c,e,f,h<br>Outcomes: b,c,d,e,f,g,<br>i,j,k | Outcomes: a,b,c,d,e,f,h,i |
| Wales | Range: 1,2,3,5,6<br>Skills: 1,2,3,4,5,6<br>Language<br>Development: 1,2,3,4,5 | Range: 1,2,3,4,6<br>Skills: 1,2,4<br>Language<br>Development: 1,2 | Range: 1,3,4,5,6,7<br>Skills: 1,2,4,5,6,7,8<br>Language<br>Development: 1,2,3,4 |
| NC KS2/NLS Y3T1 | 1c 2c 3b 4a | W11 T1 T5 | T22 |
| Born to Dance *The Story of Rudolf Nureyev* | | | |
| Scotland | Level C | Level C | Level C |
| N. Ireland | Activities: a,b,c,f,g,h,i<br>Outcomes: a,b,c,d,e,f,g | Activities: a,b,c,e,f,h<br>Outcomes: b,c,d,e,f,g,<br>i,j,k | Outcomes: a,b,c,d,e,f,h,i |
| Wales | Range: 1,2,3,5,6<br>Skills: 1,2,3,4,5,6<br>Language<br>Development: 1,2,3,4,5 | Range: 1,2,3,4,6<br>Skills: 1,2,4<br>Language<br>Development: 1,2 | Range: 1,3,4,5,6,7<br>Skills: 1,2,4,5,6,7,8<br>Language<br>Development: 1,2,3,4 |
| NC KS2/NLS Y3T1 | 1a 2c 3a 4b | W8 S7 T19 | T26 |

# Vocabulary chart

| The King<br>of Football<br>*The Story of Pelé* | Years 1-2<br>High frequency words | after again back be but could down first from had have help her him his live made many much next now one out so that then three too took were when who with would very |
|---|---|---|
| | Spelling strategies:<br>Words with -le | trouble |
| | Glossary words | announce foul hat-trick header injury international game kick-off professional footballer stadium tournament trial |
| **Arctic Hero**<br>*The Story of*<br>*Matthew Henson* | Years 1-2<br>High frequency words | about after again back be because boy but by called could first from good had helped him his how just last made make more next off old once one out over people pulled put ran so some take than their then there three time too took wanted way were when where with would |
| | Spelling strategies:<br>Verb spellings<br>that change with -ing | exploring arriving deserving giving making travelling getting setting strapping |
| | Glossary words | blizzard charr expedition frostbite hoax husky igloo Inuit meteorite North Pole the Arctic |

| | | |
|---|---|---|
| **Pioneer Girl**<br>*The Story of*<br>*Laura Ingalls*<br>*Wilder* | Years 1-2<br>High frequency words | about back big but came door from had have helped his home house how just little lived loved make many new next night now off once one our over run school so that then them there time took us very way when where with wanted ways were where why would |
| | Spelling patterns:<br>Words that change<br>with -er, -est | flater greatest older colder |
| | Glossary words | blizzard cape candy claim cornbread creek Indian pioneer prairie prairie chicken replica sap |
| **Man on the Moon**<br>*The Story of*<br>*Neil Armstrong* | Years 1-2<br>High frequency words | about after back be been by called came down first from had have here him his how just make many now off once one out over pushes put so take than that their them there three time too wanted way were when where who with would |
| | Spelling strategies:<br>Building from words<br>with similar patterns | aeronautics cosmonaut supersonic kilometres spacecraft |
| | Glossary words | aeronautics astronaut cockpit cosmonaut crater engineer gravity licence Houston Korean War Lunar Module NASA orbit quarantine satellite solar glare sputnik supersonic test pilot |
| **Titanic Survivor**<br>*The Story of*<br>*Harold Bride* | Years 1-2<br>High frequency words | about back because but called could first from had have help him his how last make man many more new night now off one our people put ran saw seen so some take than that them time too took us |
| | Spelling strategies:<br>Apostrophe for<br>contractions | "the ship's damaged" "the ship's lights" you'll couldn't didn't it's weren't hadn't that's |
| | Glossary words | Atlantic bridge deck iceberg Morse Code oarlock SOS |
| **Born to Dance**<br>*The Story of*<br>*Rudolf Nureyev* | Years 1-2<br>High frequency words | about after again back been but called came could down from help him his home how last loved night old ran that their too took very wanted were who with when where who would |
| | Spelling strategies:<br>Identify short words<br>within longer ones | brilliant countries discovered elegant fortune important potatoes theatre |
| | Glossary words | audition ballerina burly dormitory evacuate nomads rebel Second World War spy "Swinging Sixties" Tartar |

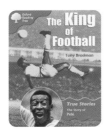

# The King of Football
## *The Story of Pelé*

### *Group and independent reading activities*

### Introducing the story

Read the "blurb" on the cover and find out what the children already know about Pelé. *Can anyone explain where Brazil is?* Find Brazil in an atlas. Read the words in the index so that everyone knows how to pronounce them. Read the words in the glossary one at a time. Ask a child to explain the word to the group. Read the definition in the book. Look through the pictures. Ask *Why do you think this book is called "The King of Football"?*

### During reading

*Observing* ● to use awareness of grammar to decipher new and unfamiliar words, e.g. to predict from the text, read on, leave a gap and return; to use these strategies in conjunction with knowledge of phonemes, word recognition, graphic knowledge and context when reading Y3T1S1

● Ask one child to read a few pages aloud to you. Notice which of the above strategies he or she uses to cope with new words. If a child pronounces a word wrongly, say "Well done, it's…"

● If a child makes four or five mistakes on one page (about 50 words) the book might be too difficult. Try a story at an earlier stage.

● If a child reads fluently with no mistakes, ask: *How did you know how to read …?* Ask them to explain the strategies they use.

### Comprehension

*Objective* **Y3T1T19** locate information using contents, index, page nos

● Ask one child to use the index to find out about the World Cup in Sweden. *Which pages should everyone turn to?* (pp10-13)

● Ask them to read these pages and tell you one fact each about Pelé at the 1958 World Cup.

● Ask another child to use the contents page to find out about goal 1000. *Which page do we need?*

● Turn to page 20 and skim-read the chapter. Make up a sentence that tells us about Pelé's thousandth goal.

- Ask the children to skim through the pages to find the page where Pelé was injured. He had to watch Brazil win a World Cup without him. When you have found the page, tell everyone else the page number. (page 18)

**Assessment points**
- Notice whether children know how to use the contents/index to find information. Could they find the entry in the list quickly?
- Were the children able to skim through pages to find the information, or did they look at pages at random?

## Using spelling strategies

**Objective**    *Y3T1W9* investigate and learn to use the spelling pattern -le.

Although "trouble" is the only -le word in the story, you can use this to generate more. Write "trouble" on the board.
- Ask the children to think of words that rhyme with "trouble": *bubble, rubble, double*. Make a class list for reference.
- Suppose you change the vowel, what can you get then? *Babble, dabble, rabble; wobble, bobble, cobble, hobble; nibble; pebble.*
- Change the consonants to -dd-, then you can have paddle, saddle; *peddle, meddle; riddle, fiddle; toddle; muddle, huddle.*
- Add more -le words as children find them in reading.
- Include -ible words: *horrible, terrible, possible.*
- Practise spelling words on your list.

**Assessment points**
- Notice whether the children understand the way you are changing the spelling patterns to make new words. Are they suggesting suitable words, or just guessing?
- Did they remember the -le pattern when learning the spellings?

## *Speaking and listening activities*

**Objectives**
1c) choose material that is relevant to the topic and the listener;
2b) ask relevant questions to clarify, extend and follow up ideas;
3d) deal politely with opposing point of view and enable the discussion to move on;
4a) create, adapt and sustain roles individually and in groups

**Cross-curricular links**
History:
*KS2 2a the ideas, beliefs, attitudes and experiences of the past*

## Responding to the book

*Why do you think that Pelé's mother didn't want him to be a footballer?*
*Pelé was small and skinny at 17, what made him special as a footballer? Why did other players foul Pelé?*
*Why is Pelé still thought of as the greatest footballer ever?*

## Personal experiences/Cross-curricular links

- Have a Circle Time discussion about great sportsmen and women. Everyone says why Pelé, or another sports person was great. Saying "He's the best" is not enough without explaining why.
- Children who do not follow sport can answer from the book.
- Others can introduce their own heroes.
- Make it a rule that you can only disagree politely. Children should be able to give a sensible reason for disagreeing.

## Role-play

- Read pages 4–7 again.
- Imagine a discussion about Pelé being a footballer.
- What might his mother have said? *"You'll never earn any money at that game." "You'll always be travelling and never see us."* etc.
- Think of Pelé's answers: *"It's the only thing I'm any good at." "I'm desperate to be a footballer."* etc.
- Ask two volunteers to invent a conversation about it.
- Applaud the performance, then ask two more children.
- Praise children for speaking with realistic expression.

## *Writing*

| Objective | Y3T1W5 identify mis-spelt words in own writing |
|---|---|

*Pelé's first World Cup*
- Ask the children to write a short account of how Brazil won the 1958 World Cup from pages 10–15.
- Point out that many of the spellings they will need are available from the story.
- As they write, remind children to reread and check their work.
- Ask children to underline any words they are not sure of.
- Ask children to use dictionaries and the story to check the words.

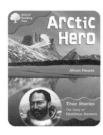

# Arctic Hero
## *The Story of Matthew Henson*

### *Group and independent reading activities*

### Introducing the story

Use the information on the cover to decide what the book is going to be about. *Where is the Arctic? Where is the Antarctic? Look at the pictures. What kind of personality do you think an explorer has? Have you heard of any other explorers?*

Read the words in the index together. Read the words in the glossary. Ask if anyone can define the word before you read the definition in the book.

### During reading

| Observing | ● to take account of grammar and punctuation when reading aloud Y3T1S2 |

- Ask one child to read a chapter aloud.
- If commas and exclamation marks are ignored, read the sentence yourself, showing how a sentence should be read.
- Praise the child for working out any new words without help.

### Comprehension

| Objective | **Y3T1T1** to compare a range of story settings and to select words and phrases that describe scenes |

- Find page 7. Look through the text to find the words that describe the jungle and the Arctic. (sticky heat, bitter cold) Ask the children to explain why "sticky" and "bitter" are well chosen.
  Read page 15 again. *What was holding up their progress? Why were blizzards a problem? Why was melting ice a problem?*
- Look at page 21. *Why did their sledges break? What other problem did they have with ice?*
- Read the first sentence on page 22. *How does this sentence help us to understand what it was like?*
- Page 24 tells us what it needs to be like to travel quickly in the Arctic. *Which sentence explains this?*
- Find a danger of the jungle on page 6 and a danger of the Arctic on page 11. *What other dangers might there be?*

| | |
|---|---|
| **Assessment points** | • Notice whether the children could pick out the words and phrases that described the conditions.<br>• Could they explain why these words helped us understand the places? |

## Using spelling strategies

| | |
|---|---|
| *Objective* | **Y3T1W8** how the spelling of verbs alter when -ing is added |

- Find "exploring" on page 7. Ask the children to spell "explore". *What do they notice when -ing is added?*
- Find "deserved" and "given" on page 27. *How would you spell "deserve" and "give"? How would you spell "deserving" and "giving"? Can you think of a rule to explain what happens when you add -ing?*
- Test the rule with "make", "have" and "race".
- Find "travelling" on page 12. How do you spell "travel"? What do you notice about "travelling"?
- Find "getting" on page 19. Talk about the spelling of "get" and "getting". Find "setting" on page 20. Can you think of a rule that explains the spelling of these words?
- Make a list of words to test the rule: *sit, fit, let, run, chat, strap.* Ask the children to spell each word with -ing. Think of more verbs that fit this rule.

| | |
|---|---|
| **Assessment points** | • Could the children recognize a spelling pattern when adding -ing?<br>• Who could express a general rule?<br>• Who could think of appropriate examples? |

## *Speaking and listening activities*

| | |
|---|---|
| *Objectives* | 1c) choose material that is relevant to the topic and listeners;<br>2a) identify key points in a discussion and evaluate;<br>3b) vary contributions to suit the activity and purpose;<br>4c) use dramatic techniques to explore characters and issues |
| *Cross-curricular links* | History:<br>*KS2 2a the ideas, beliefs, attitudes and experiences of men, women and children in the past*<br>Geography:<br>*Knowledge and understanding of places: 3a identify and describe what places are like* |

### Responding to the story

*When did Matthew stop being a servant?* (page 6)
*What did Robert and Matthew learn from the Inuit people?*
*(page 9)*
*What is frostbite?* (pages 13/14)
*Why weren't they treated as heroes when they got back to*
*America?* (page 26)
*Why did Matthew not get a medal until he was an old man?*
*(page 27)*

### Personal experiences/Cross-curricular links

- Make a list of all the hazards of being in the Arctic.
- Think of any good things. *What did the explorers achieve? Who did they make friends with? What did they learn?*
- In a Circle Time, say the best and worst things about the journey.
- When everyone has contributed, decide whether such journeys are worth it. Do *you think they are too dangerous? Do you think people should discover new places and learn from other people?*

## *Writing*

| Objective | Y3T1T13 collect words and phrases in order to write poems and short descriptions |
|---|---|

- Ask children if they remember to read words/phrases about the ice and cold.
- Write phrases on the board: "bitter cold" (page 7), "frostbitten" (page 13), "blizzards", "melting ice", (page 15), "so jagged it broke their sledges" (page 21), "the ice creaked and moaned" (page 22)
- Think of some more words to describe the cold and desolation, e.g. *howling wind, icy breath, numb fingers.*
- Children write a description of "The Arctic" or an acrostic using the letters of ARCTIC as the first letter in each line.

# Pioneer Girl
## *The Story of Laura Ingalls Wilder*
### *Group and independent reading activities*

### Introducing the story

Read the titles and the "blurb". *Have you heard of Laura Ingalls Wilder? Have you seen "Little House on the Prairie on television? What is it about?* Read the words and definitions in the glossary. *Which words do you know already?* Read the chapter titles.

### During reading

**Observing** ● *note where commas occur in reading and discuss their function in helping the reader Y3T2S6*

● Ask one child to read a chapter. Notice whether the child uses punctuation to help phrase his or her reading. Does the child notice commas and use them to improve expression?

● Use a long sentence with commas (such as "Soon after the wolves came..." on page 14) to show how commas let you read and understand each part separately.

● Read a sentence without pausing for commas so that children can hear the difference.

● Praise children for using punctuation to read with expression.

### Comprehension

**Objective** ● *Y3T2T3* identify and discuss main and recurring characters, evaluate their behaviour and justify views

Talk about what you have found out about Laura and her family.
*What did her father do to get food?* (page 15, page 21)
*How did the family get furniture?* (page 14)
*When was her mother very brave?* (page 15) What did she do?
*Was Laura bullied at school? What happened?* (page 20)
*What happened to Mary?* (page 21)
*Why was Laura shy when they moved to a town?* (page 23)
*What have you learned about pioneers?*

**Assessment** ● Did the children understand the pioneers were self-sufficient?
**points** ● Could they justify their comments about characters by referring to the story?

## Using spelling strategies

**Objective** ● **W8** how words change when -er and -est are added.

● Use words from the story and make a table:

| adjective | more | most |
|:---:|:---:|:---:|
| | later | |
| dark | | |
| safe | | |
| | | greatest |

● Ask the children to scan the text for more adjectives: *hard, lucky, thin, sad, cold, weak, wild, happy*. Fill in the table.
● Ask the children to spell the words with -er and -est added.
● Show how the spelling changes for words ending -y, e.g. *luckier, luckiest*.
● Show spelling changes where a single vowel is followed by a single consonant, e.g. *thin, sad*.
● Talk about words where adding -er and -est doesn't sound right, e.g. *good, bad, dangerous*.

**Assessment points**
● Can the children recognize adjectives, or are they suggesting other parts of speech?
● Did they understand the spelling pattern?
● Could they spell words to be added to the chart?

## Speaking and listening activities

**Objectives**
1a) use vocabulary/syntax to communicate complex meanings;
2c) respond to others appropriately;
3a) make relevant contributions and take turns in discussion;
4b) use character, action and narrative to convey story, themes, emotions, ideas in plays they devise and script

**Cross-curricular links**
History:
*KS2 2a the ideas, beliefs, attitudes and experiences of men, women and children in the past*

### Responding to the story/Cross-curricular links

- *Why did the author have so many stories about her childhood?*
- *Why did the family move from place to place?*
- *Why did they nearly starve one winter?*
- *What did you need to be good at to be a pioneer?*
- *Would you have enjoyed being a child pioneer? Why?*

### Personal experiences

Ask if the children have ever been camping. *What were the best and worst things about camping? Where did they wash?*
Compare camping with being a pioneer. *What was worse than camping? What would have been even better than camping?*
Compare being in the woods and being in a town. *What would be better in the town? What would not be so good?*
*Would you rather live in the country or in the town? Why?*

### Role-play

- Read page 20 again. Talk about Nellie Oleson. She was richer than Laura and had nicer clothes. Laura says she was cruel to her. What do you think Nellie might have said and done?

## *Writing*

| *Objective* | **T17** make clear notes through identifying key words, phrases or sentences in reading |
| --- | --- |

*Laura's Adventures* notes about what happened in each house.

- Make a list of the houses and a phrase or sentence to remind you of an adventure there, e.g.
- Little House in the Big woods – Ma slapped a bear
- Little House on the Prairie – Pa hunting, Indians, cornbread
- Use the notes to retell an adventure to the group, e.g. "It was when we were living in the big woods. One night Ma…"

# Man on the Moon
## *The Story of Neil Armstrong*

### *Group and independent reading activities*

### Introducing the story

Read the information on the cover and the introduction. Find out what the children know about the moon. *Is it possible to live there? What do people need to be able to breathe there?* Read through the words in the index to check pronunciation of the names. Read through the words in the glossary. Some children might like to explain the meanings of words they already know before reading the definition.

### During reading

| | |
|---|---|
| *Observing* | ● rehearse and improve performance, taking note of punctuation and meaning Y3T2S6 |

- Ask one child to read aloud.
- As the child reads notice whether he or she is taking account of punctuation and using the appropriate expression.
- If commas are ignored, reread the sentence yourself.
- Show how commas help both the reader and the listener understand the sentence.
- Ask each child to choose a page that has commas in sentences. Practise reading that page silently.
- Take turns to read your page to the group with expression.

### Comprehension

| | |
|---|---|
| *Objective* | **T7** describe and sequence key incidents in a variety of ways |

- Turn to page 7. Ask the children to find Neil Armstrong's job at this time.
- Begin a flowchart that shows Neil Armstrong's achievements. Decide what to call your flowchart.
- Write "1962 test Pilot for NASA"
- On the following page find out what happened next. Ask the children to tell you what to write. Draw another arrow.
- The next achievement is on page 10. Ask the children to find it.
- Find the next item on page 19.
- Turn to page 21 for the next important moment.
- Pages 22–25 tell us what happened next

- Decide what to put for the final item.
- Reread your notes to check that they make sense.

*Assessment points*
- Could the children identify the information they needed?
- Could they suggest the wording for you to write?

## Using spelling strategies

*Objective*
Y3T2W6 use independent spelling strategies including building from words with similar patterns and meanings

- Find "telephone" on page 24. Ask the children to tell you how to spell other words that begin tele-, such as "television" and "telescope".
- Find "kilometres" on page 13. Think of and spell other words that begin with kilo-, e.g. "kilogram".
- Find "aeronautics" and "cosmonaut" in the glossary. Notice which letters are the same in both words. Use a dictionary to find words beginning with naut-.
- Find "supersonic" in the glossary. Look for super- in a dictionary. Find some more words they recognize, such as "superman", "superintendent", "supervise".

*Assessment points*
- Were the children aware of similar patterns in different words?
- Could they use the pattern to spell other words?

## *Speaking and listening activities*

*Objectives*
1c) choose material that is relevant to the topic and the listener;
2b) ask relevant questions to clarify, extend and follow up ideas;
3a) make contributions relevant to the topic and take turns in discussion;
4a) create, adapt and sustain different roles, individually and in groups

*Cross-curricular links*
History:
*KS2 2a the ideas, beliefs, attitudes and experiences of men, women and children in the past*

### Responding to the story/Cross-curricular links
- *How many people flew in Apollo 11?*
- *Why did only two of them walk on the moon?*

- *What was the famous sentence Neil spoke when he stepped onto the moon?*
- *What did it mean?*
- *Why did they have to stay in quarantine when they got back to Earth?*

### Personal experiences
- *Why do you think Neil Armstrong wanted to go the moon?*
- *Why were Neil and his crew brave?*
- *Do you think it was an easy way to become famous?*
- *What would you like about a trip to the moon? What would frighten you?*
- *What is exciting about space travel?*

### Role-play
- Discuss questions that newspaper reporters would have asked the crew when they got back.
- Think of the different roles of the three men: Neil was first on the moon, and Buzz was second. Michael Collins had to stay in the command module, so he went all that way and didn't have the chance to walk on the moon.
- Ask three volunteers to be Neil, Buzz and Michael.
- Take turns to ask each of the crew questions.

## *Writing*

| Objective | **Y3T2T7** describe and sequence key incidents through making story boards |
|---|---|

- Use the sequence of events written in the Comprehension section.
- Ask the children to fold a sheet of A4 paper into four. Using both sides of the sheet this gives eight pictures from the story.
- Using the illustrations in the book and their own ideas, ask the children to illustrate eight events from the book. They can use the notes from the Comprehension sequence to annotate their pictures.
- Ask the children to use their storyboards to retell the story of Neil Armstrong to the rest of the class.

# Titanic Survivor
## *The Story of Harold Bride*
### *Group and independent reading activities*

### Introducing the story

Read the blurb and talk about the Titanic. Has anyone seen the film? What happened to the ship? How long ago was it? Read the words in the index to check pronunciation of names. Read the words in the glossary. Ask children if they can explain any of the words without reading the definition. Read the chapter titles on the contents page. Predict what will happen in the chapter "The Terrible Truth".

### During reading

*Observing* ●  to use awareness of grammar to decipher new and unfamiliar words, e.g. to predict from the text, read on, leave a gap and return; to use these strategies in conjunction with knowledge of phonemes, word recognition, graphic knowledge and context when reading Y3T3S1

- ● As a child reads, notice the strategies used for unfamiliar words.
- ● Remind children to read past a word they do not know, then go back and use phonics to give more clues to a word that would fit.
- ● Praise children for using the sense of the sentence, phonic patterns and information in the pictures to work out new words.

### Comprehension

*Objective*  **Y3T3T5** discuss (i) characters' feelings, (ii) behaviour, (iii) relationships referring to the text and making judgments

- ● Ask the children what they have found out about Harold Bride.
  *How old was Harold? What was his job?* (page 4)
  *Who was his friend?* (page 7)
  *Why weren't they worried at first?* (page 10)
  *When did they begin to be afraid?* (page 14)
  *What did Harold do to help his friend?* (pages 16, 18)
  *How do you think Harold felt under the lifeboat?* (page 21)
  *Was he safe when he got into a boat?* (page 24)
  *Was Harold happy to survive?* (page 28)
  *What did Harold do on the Carpathia?* (page 29)

| | |
|---|---|
| **Assessment points** | • Who could remember facts about the story without looking back at the text?<br>• Could the children scan the page and find the right information?<br>• Who could express an opinion about Harold Bride? Could they back up their opinion by incidents from the story? |

## Using spelling strategies

| | |
|---|---|
| **Objective** | **Y3T3W11** use the apostrophe to spell contracted forms |

• Ask the children to scan through the book to find words with apostrophes. Make a list. ("the ship's damaged", "the ship's lights", you'll, couldn't ,didn't, it's, we've, weren't, hadn't, that's)

• First find all the apostrophes that show possession: "the ship's lights", "the passengers' families", "Phillips' shoulders".

Then make a list of all the words with n't. *Which letter is missing? What would the longer way of writing this be?*

• Find words with 'll , what is the 'll sound short for?

Find a word with 've. What word is 've short for? Say could've, would've, might've in two words each time.

• Find the words with apostrophe s. Say the two words.

• Reread your lists to check that everyone knows what the abbreviated forms are short for.

• Finally you might like to scan the story for plurals with s: seas, decks, friends, lights, legs. Reinforce the point that plurals with s do not need an apostrophe.

| | |
|---|---|
| **Assessment points** | • Note whether children are aware of the words that are abbreviated by apostrophes.<br>• Does everyone understand that 've is short for "have" and should not be written or spoken as "of"? |

## Speaking and listening activities

| | |
|---|---|
| **Objectives** | 1c) choose material that is relevant to the topic and the listeners;<br>2c) recall and represent important features of a reading;<br>3b) vary contributions to suit the activity and purpose;<br>4a) create and sustain different roles, individually and in groups |
| **Cross-curricular links** | PSHE and Citizenship:<br>*4b to think about the lives of people living in other places/times* |

## Responding to the story

Ask the following questions to find out what children remember:
*What was Harold Bride's job?* (page 4)
*Where was the Titanic travelling to?* (page 50)
*What caused the accident?* (page 9)
*How did Harold survive?* (page 20)

## Personal experiences/Cross-curricular links

Talk about ships, ferries and boats that the children have travelled on. *Did you enjoy the trip? What happened? What did Harold and Jack do that night that made them heroes? Can you think of ways that we can do ordinary things every day to help other people?*

## Role-play

- Talk about what other members of the crew might have seen and done, e.g. helped get children into the lifeboats, helped old people who couldn't walk very well, announced to the passengers that they should come up to the deck.
- Demonstrate how to take on the role of a member of the crew of Titanic. Using the information in the story say in three or four sentences what happened on that night.
- Ask volunteers to imagine the same thing. They can use the same role or a different one. Remember to say "I", not "he" or "she".

## *Writing*

| Objective | T22 recount the same event in a variety of ways, e.g. a letter |
|---|---|

- Imagine that Harold is writing to the family of his friend Jack.
- Make a list of things you would mention:
  A good friend, shared a cabin (page 7)
  Worked hard for the passengers (page 8)
  Went on sending messages as the ship sank (page 17)
  Jack was a hero (page 30)
- Use these notes to write a letter. Decide who to write to.
- Remember to say how sad you are that Jack died. Tell the family that they should be proud of Jack.

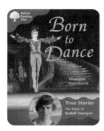

# Born to Dance
## *The Story of Rudolf Nureyev*

### *Group and independent reading activities*

### Introducing the story

Read the title and the information on the cover. Ask the children if they have heard of Nureyev? *What do they know about him?* Read the words in the index and the glossary. Ask children to explain the meanings of words they know. Read the chapter headings. *What do you think will happen?*

### During reading

| | |
|---|---|
| *Observing* ● | *become aware of the use of commas in marking the grammatical boundaries within a sentence Y3T3S7* |

- Remind children to break longer words down into syllables and use phonics to help read them.
- Notice whether children are aware of commas in sentences.
- If children pass over commas, reread the sentence yourself to show how it should sound and explain how they help.

### Comprehension

| | |
|---|---|
| *Objective* | *Y3T3T19* summarize orally in one sentence the content of a passage or text and the main point it is making |

- Reread the first paragraph on page 4. *What are the most important facts on this page? How can we put them into one sentence?* Write the agreed sentence on a board, e.g. "Rudolf Nureyev was born in Russia in 1938."
- Read page 8. Find two important facts about Rudolf's childhood. (poor, loved music) Think of a sentence that mentions these two facts. Write the sentence for the group to read again later.
- Read page 10 to find out what Rudolf liked about ballet. Think of a sentence that explains it.
- Read page 14. *What was Rudolf's ambition? What did he do to achieve it?* Try to put this information into one sentence.
- Read page 17. *What is important on this page?* Make up a sentence that includes where Rudolf was going and who was going to be watching him.

- Read all the sentences so far. *Do they tell us about Rudolf's life?*
- Ask children to put more facts into sentences by reading pages 18, 21, 23 and 25.

<table>
<tr><td>Assessment points</td><td>● Were the children able to select the most important facts?<br>● Who could suggest a sentence that summed up the paragraph?</td></tr>
</table>

## Using spelling strategies

**Objective**    **Y3T3W8** identify short words within longer words as an aid to spelling

- Use "everyone" as an example. Ask children to search for words inside words. The letters must be next to each other, such as "very". They could suggest "eve", "every", "very", "on", "one".
- Write a list of words from the story: *brilliant, countries, discovered, elegant, fortune, important, potatoes, theatre.*
- Ask the children to copy the list and find at least one smaller word inside each longer one.
- Ask children to close their eyes and spell one word each. Talk about the way the small words help to spell the longer ones.

**Assessment points**    ● Could the children find short words inside the longer ones?
   ● Could they spell long words, using short words as clues?

## Speaking and listening activities

**Objectives**    1a) use vocabulary/syntax to communicate more complex meanings;
2c) recall and represent important features of a reading;
3a) make relevant contributions and take turns in discussion;
4b) use character, action and narrative to convey story themes, emotions and ideas in plays they devise and script

**Cross-curricular links**    History:
*KS2 2a the ideas, beliefs, attitudes and experiences of in the past*

### Responding to the story/Cross-curricular links
*Why were spies watching Rudolf?*
*Why did he need to get to London?*
*Who helped Rudolf escape?*
*What happened in London?*

## Personal experiences

Talk about rules. *What are some of the school's rules? Why do we have them? Do you disagree with any rules? Why?*
*Which rule was Rudolf breaking?* (Not allowed to speak to foreigners.) *Was this a good rule? What do you think about it? Can you think of a reason why a country would have this rule?*

## Role-play

- Reread pages 22, 23 and 24. Ask for volunteers to act out this scene. You will need Clara, Rudolf, two spies, and some policemen.
- *What are the spies going to be doing? Will they say anything?*
- *What will Rudolf do? What will he say to Clara?*
- *What will Clara do? What will she say to the Police?*
- *Will the police say anything to Clara? What will they do next?*
- *What did Clara do next? What did Rudolf do?*

## *Writing*

**Objective**      **Y3T3T26** summarize in writing the content of a passage or text and the main point it is making

*Dangerous Behaviour*
- Read pages 16–17 again to remind the children how Rudolf was breaking the rules in Paris. Then read chapter 5.
- Talk about Rudolf's behaviour. *Why was it dangerous? What did the spies tell the Secret Police?*
- Ask the children to write their own version of this chapter in fewer words, e.g. four or five sentences.
- Read all the summaries. Talk about the different versions. *Which ones give us the most information in the fewest words?*

## Links to other Oxford Reading Tree titles

Branch Library Non-fiction Stages 8-10 *Reds* packs A and B

Branch Library Biographies: *What's Their Story?*
Pack A Stages 10-13; pack B Stages 10-14

Fact Finders units D, E and F

# OXFORD
UNIVERSITY PRESS

Great Clarendon Street, Oxford OX2 6DP

Oxford University Press is a department of the University of Oxford.
It furthers the University's objective of excellence in research,
scholarship, and education by publishing worldwide in

Oxford New York

Auckland Cape Town Dar es Salaam Hong Kong Karachi
Kuala Lumpur Madrid Melbourne Mexico City Nairobi
New Delhi Shanghai Taipei Toronto

With offices in

Argentina Austria Brazil Chile Czech Republic France Greece
Guatemala Hungary Italy Japan Poland Portugal Singapore
South Korea Switzerland Thailand Turkey Ukraine Vietnam

Oxford is a registered trade mark of Oxford University Press
in the UK and in certain other countries

British Library Cataloguing in Publication Data

Data available

Cover illustrations Alex Brychta

Teacher's Notes: ISBN 10: 019 919698 2
              ISBN 13: 978 019 919698 2

10 9 8 7 6

Page make-up by IFA Design Ltd, Plymouth, Devon

Printed in China by Imago